M000211476

I want to be creative

*for ARH, who reignited
my creativity, with love*

Other books in the *I want to...* series:

I want to sleep
I want to be calm
I want to be organised
I want to be confident
I want to be happy

I want to be creative

THINKING, LIVING AND WORKING MORE CREATIVELY

—————— BY ——————

Harriet Griffey

hardie grant books

Contents

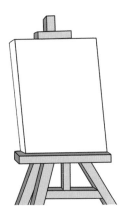

What is creativity?

We are all capable of creativity, whatever we do and however we live our lives, just as long as we are open to imagination and are flexible about new ideas and possibilities.

We know it adds value to and is actively sought in the workplace, but creativity is also valuable in its own right and has an important place in the lives of all of us. Exploring our creativity through the arts, literature and sport, for example, enhances how we live and even improves and supports our mental health.

Creativity is a wild mind and a disciplined eye.

DOROTHY PARKER, WRITER

'The future belongs to a different kind of person,' says Daniel Pink, author of *A Whole New Mind: Why Right-Brainers Will Rule the Future*. 'Designers, inventors, teachers, storytellers – creative and empathetic right-brain thinkers whose abilities mark the fault line between who gets ahead and who doesn't.'

Although some personality types are more open to harnessing creative possibilities, it's something we can all cultivate, exploit and enjoy either through recognisably creative activities like music, painting, cooking or writing, or in the way we develop ideas or approach problem solving, whether that's alone or in collaboration with others.

Creativity isn't an occupation. It's a preoccupation. It invents, perfects and defines our world. It explains and entertains us.
John Hegarty, founding Creative Partner, Bartle Bogle Hegarty

---

Exploring our personal creativity could mean a whole new way of thinking and enhancing what we do, and its positive impact is increasingly recognised in all areas of life and work. It's about using and extending our imaginations, looking outside ourselves for inspiration and, very often, finding that our most creative ideas occur when we least expect them. We also need to be willing to go beyond what psychologists call 'functional fixedness', to explore and play with ideas that might – or might not – work. It's not necessarily about trying harder at something to achieve a creative outcome, either, but trying differently.

Creativity is intelligence having fun. *Albert Einstein, scientist*

Creativity is an expression of yourself and the way in which you choose to live your life. You can express your creativity in all sorts of ways, from the way you dress to what you cook, to the books you read and the music you listen to. When something interests you, you can explore it further by taking a class or joining a group of enthusiasts.

A dictionary definition of creativity: 'The use of imagination or original ideas to create something', and this isn't a bad starting point to help us consider what creativity is. What can be taken from this is there is a direct link between an idea and the use of that idea to create *something*; as a consequence of that idea, something tangible will be brought into existence. Creativity is, therefore, a process by which something comes into existence. Creativity isn't, then, an abstract concept but something that leads to a tangible outcome.

Creativity lets you explore what can be difficult to express, our emotions for example, perhaps through art, music or creative writing. Nourishing your creativity can also help you be more creative when handling problems and finding solutions, helping you see the world in more than one way. Take a photography class, keep a journal, take up drawing, dancing, cooking – anything that expresses who you are and what you feel in a way that's fun and gives you a sense of satisfaction. It's also worth remembering that creativity requires not just imagination but also something else to arrive at its outcome. Extending this further, we can see that creativity is a combination of several different things: talent, maybe; imagination, probably; application, definitely; and effort, for sure.

The benefits of creativity

As someone once said, creativity is 1 per cent inspiration and 99 per cent perspiration, and examples of the results of the perspiration of creativity are very evident in James Dyson's story. He was dissatisfied by the lack of suction in his vacuum cleaner and came up with an idea that would improve it using cyclonic technology, which he had noticed was effective in removing sawdust in a mill he visited that used centrifugal separators. Between 1979 and 1984 he developed 5127 prototypes, but it would take almost another ten years before he was successful. By 2001, however, he had a 47 per cent market share of the upright vacuum cleaner market. At school, Dyson excelled at long-distance running. He said, 'I was quite good at it, not because I was physically good, but because I had more determination. I learnt determination from it.' From school he went to art college before moving into engineering. This diversity of influences, his openness to ideas, and his imagination, determination and willingness to explore and make mistakes all demonstrate what it takes to be creative.

If you feel you would benefit from including more personal creativity in your life, look for ways in which to do this. Read a book, take photographs or join a photography group, keep a journal, take up drawing, pottery, dancing, cooking – anything that gives you a way to explore greater creativity that expresses who you are and what you feel, in a way that's fun and both personally and professionally rewarding.

The value of creativity

Creativity is of personal value to the enrichment of our lives, but it can also be of huge, measurable economic value in business. It's not just in the creative industries that being creative can be instrumental in bringing about good results, either. Increasingly, whatever the working sector or industry, creativity is seen as having, or adding, value to everything we do. Being open to ideas and new sources of information means we bring more to the table when it comes to addressing problems or innovating ways of solving them. If something doesn't work out, it's seldom a question of trying harder – but rather trying differently. And that's where creativity comes in.

In 2010, IBM conducted a survey of 1500 CEOs (across 33 industries and 60 countries) and discovered that they rated creativity as more important than discipline, integrity or vision for the successful navigation of an increasingly complex world. And prior to that, an OECD (Organisation for Economic Cooperation and Development) working paper had identified 'creativity and innovation' as core 21st-century competencies. And this desire for creativity as a necessity occurred around the same time that a decrease in creative thinking scores (based on the Torrance Tests of Creative Thinking) was identified even while IQ scores in general had risen.

It's not always easy to see how creativity can contribute to business, especially in a climate of caution, and particularly when creativity can be seen as a disruptive element, demanding both experimentation and risk. In addition, there is greater complexity in the way we work today, and this is combined with speed – a demand for things to be executed fast. It takes an ability to think laterally and in divergent ways to come up with solutions where constraints are seen as challenges, and this comes from an ability to think creatively. Remember when people talked about 'thinking outside the box'? This is a bit like that: only today there are more boxes and they are of multiple sizes and colours.

Creativity involves the breaking out of established patterns in order to look at things in a different way.

EDWARD DE BONO, PSYCHOLOGIST, WRITER & PIONEER OF 'LATERAL THINKING'

Proust, Puccini, Picasso ... and Prada

What comes next is applying creativity in a way that drives business. Creativity is more than self-actualisation, where we discover our inner Proust, Puccini or Picasso, and it's more like Miuccia Prada, who took her PhD in political science and her interest in theatre and mime and put it into handbag design, and then her family's business, saying, 'Art is for expressing ideas and expressing a vision. My job is to sell.' That may smack of self-deprecation, but she has successfully harnessed her creativity to this end and along the way was awarded the first International Designer of the Year accolade at the British Fashion Awards in 2013.

Productivity

Even though there is risk implied it doing something differently – after all, it might not work out – creativity can lead to greater productivity. A great example of this is Henry Ford's production line. Manufacturing cars was a slow business until he worked out that a production line would make the process more efficient – once he'd worked out how to do it – and he was right. His innovative idea came from a problem for which he sought a solution and it started with a question: how can I do this?

The creative brain

The general consensus is that there isn't really any such thing as a creative brain, not in isolation anyway; it's much more a question of taking what we have and using it creatively. What we have may be imagination that finds an outlet, but it may also include seeking to find those things that stimulate creativity and feed curiosity, raising questions of 'What if?' for us to answer. This is open to us all.

Creativity often consists of merely turning up what is already there. Did you know that right and left shoes were thought up only a little more than a century ago?

Bernice Fitz-Gibbon, advertising executive

Only connect

There is some agreement, however, that creativity is related to the neuroplasticity of the brain, the flexible response and adaptation that the brain's neural pathways make in response to stimulation. Neural pathways, the connections between them, and the connections these make between the different parts of the brain, all play a part in the brain's inclination towards creativity. Exposure to different stimuli – new sounds, sights and sensations – create connections in the brain via the synapses, the points of connection, between the neurons. The more neurons, the more neural pathways and more synapses, and the greater the opportunity to spark ideas and solutions: and this neuroplasticity is capable of generation and regeneration throughout our lives, given the right stimulus.

Right brain/left brain

The function of the right side of the brain is generally related to visual comprehension and spatial information, while the left side tends towards language and logic: but they work together, not separately.

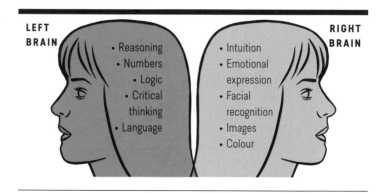

LEFT BRAIN
- Reasoning
- Numbers
- Logic
- Critical thinking
- Language

RIGHT BRAIN
- Intuition
- Emotional expression
- Facial recognition
- Images
- Colour

Male v. female

Yes, there is a difference. That's not to say that one is better than the other, but male and female brains do connect differently. In 2013 the University of Pennsylvania published research based on the analysis of almost 1,000 MRI scans of the brains of males and females aged between 8 and 22. Researchers analysing the scans found that male brains have more connections within each hemisphere, but female brains have more connections between the left and right hemispheres. This meant that there was greater potential for connections between the more intuitive right brain and the more logical left brain.

What does an idea look like?

An idea is generated by the network of connections in the brain, and is the result of a number of different things. 'You need memory but you also need speech and language,' says neuroscientist Professor Faraneh Vargha-Khadem. 'Thoughts are fleeting so the only way that we can capture our own thoughts is if we either talked about them, wrote them down or signed them into physical reality. The expression of ideas make us human.'

The word idea comes from the Greek *idein*, which means 'to see', as if we might see the outcome of our thoughts. Ideas can actually be seen to happen on an MRI scan as they generate blood flow in the brain, which then 'lights up' the area of the brain that has been stimulated. When we think of, for example, a verb associated with a noun, connections are made. Given the noun 'map' and being asked to think of a verb associated with it, we may think of 'to travel', and the creation of this idea, and its association to others, literally lights up areas of the brain.

What next?

An idea is not enough; we have to act on it, explore it and develop it in order to create something. We may have a genetic predisposition toward a certain talent, skill or ability – having perfect pitch, for example, may make us more inclined towards expressing ourselves through music – but unless we use it, we will never have anything tangible to show for it. This is what creativity is.

To think creatively, we must be able to look afresh at what we normally take for granted.

GEORGE F. KNELLER,
AUTHOR OF THE ART & SCIENCE OF CREATIVITY

What inhibits creativity?

Sometimes, however creative we aspire or aim to be, our creativity is inhibited. A number of things can cause this, but inhibition can often come from the ways in which we think about what it is we are trying to achieve and from a place of restriction.

Self-censorship

If you have a voice in your head that constantly tells you that something is impossible, that you can't do something because perhaps you don't know how, or that what you're attempting to do can never be good enough, then this sort of self-censorship will inhibit your efforts. So, for every internal voice that says 'can't', 'shouldn't', 'not good enough', remind yourself that one of the core features of creativity is exploration, a willingness to try and an acceptance that sometimes it won't necessarily go the way you planned, and that you won't always succeed.

Remind yourself that creativity is both a process and a means to an end: how you get there is not writ in stone, nor does it have to be done in a particular way, and the only inhibition is an internal, rather than an external voice.

Functional fixedness

An inhibition of creativity can sometimes come from the way in which we think about things and this includes being rigid or inflexible in our thinking – getting stuck with an idea that there is only one way to approach something or use an object. 'Functional fixedness' is a technical term that comes from Gestalt psychology and means that the way we think about an object, and only using it for the purpose for which it was originally designed, can limit us.

For example, an infant wouldn't have any idea of what a plastic tea strainer was, but would explore it in a number of ways – chewing it, banging it, looking through it, throwing it, maybe even trying to scoop water with it – learning about its use along the way. Only when seeing an adult using it to strain tea leaves might the use for which it was designed be understood. It's not difficult to see how we can become fixed in our thinking: as we move from childhood to adulthood we can lose the sense of exploration and play that frees our creative minds – and then, a tea strainer is always just a tea strainer. Some creative types never stop responding to the world around them in a flexible way. Picasso, for example, went through an artistic phase of making sculpture from 'found objects' – his sculpture of a bull's head made from a bicycle seat and handlebars is a case in point. He saw the two items and they spoke to him of another image, which he recreated in artistic form.

Fear of failure

We've all heard about 'writers' block' and the fear of the blank page: but what is that fear – which can affect any form of creativity – about? It is often a fear of failure, but can also be a fear of others' lack of approval, or even ridicule, if we attempt something which we are not sure will be successful. We don't want to be laughed at or have our efforts dismissed. We may even desire or seek approval in order to succeed. All of these attitudes can get in the way of just putting one metaphorical foot in front of the other and exploring the possibilities of creativity that can be open to us.

Creativity is something we can all improve at ... it's about daring to learn from our mistakes.

JAMES DYSON, BRITISH INVENTOR

Failure is built into creativity ... the creative act involves this element of 'newness' and 'experimentalism', then one must expect and accept the possibility of failure.

SAUL BASS, ARTIST

> **So many of us believe in perfection, which ruins everything
> else, because perfection is not only the enemy of the good;
> it's also the enemy of the realistic, the possible, and the fun.**
> *Rebecca Solnit, writer & social commentator*

Understanding that creativity is as much about the process as the
outcome, even though the two are related, and that this process is often an
exploratory one, can be a useful way to free up the self-imposed restrictions
from a fear of failure.

Forget perfection

What is perfection anyway? If you remember that creativity is a process of
exploration, then nothing can be perfect – and this is not what you're trying
to achieve anyway. Often in the process, you reach a stage where it is good
enough – rather than perfect – and this allows you the chance to build on
it and explore further. Often, too, the pursuit of perfection is a disguise for
insecurity or a desire for recognition from others. Either in its pursuit or in
its assessment, we often make a judgement about perfection in accordance
with someone else's standards, and this can be extremely limiting.

Imagine if the only standards for art were those of Leonardo da Vinci.
It is perfect in its way, but then all art would be the same, unlike the
wonderful diversity of work we actually experience today and which
continues to develop in its expression. Likewise, if the only example of
perfection in music was the music of Mozart, and everyone aspired to that,
music would become very limited. It is in its diversity and willingness to
explore that creativity transcends the limitations of perfection. So start
the process of exploration with no attachment to the idea of perfection,
because there's a huge difference between aspiring to someone else's ideal
of perfection and making your own unique contribution.

Creative processes

It's not just what we know or think about something that can be creative, it's *how* we think about it. What's interesting about this, and how it relates to the creative process, is that we can change our thinking process and actually learn to think more creatively. It's easy to stick with a certain way of thinking – this is true across all areas of life – and we sometime choose to stay in unhelpful patterns of thinking. But it's also true, as witnessed by the effectiveness of cognitive behavioural therapy (CBT), that we can change the way we think. First, it's useful to consider some of the ways in which we do think, identifying them in order to address this and start to think more creatively.

Convergent thinking

This is the sort of thinking that fixes on finding the best possible single answer to a question or a problem. This works very well for maths or science and other certainties, but this sort of approach can be very literal, with little room for ambiguity or development outside its immediate arena.

Divergent thinking

This is how we think about things where there are multiple possible answers to a question or problem. Not everyone is comfortable with this style of thinking and it can seem a recipe for muddle and delay; but if it is well managed, it can elicit solutions as if from nowhere. There is often the sense of a 'gut feeling' being involved when, in fact, that gut feeling has arisen from a soup of knowledge and ideas, with the right solution percolating through.

Combine the two

Convergent thinking is great for working out the sum of the internal angles of a triangle, while divergent thinking is better for identifying the ten possible uses for a piece of string. Often, it's a combination of these two ways of thinking that work best. This is why working in teams, bringing different ways of thinking to the table, along with experience and information and knowledge, can be effective. But even when you are working alone, being aware of and using these different ways of thinking can enhance creativity.

Incubation

Related to 'gut feeling' is incubation, recognised
by psychologists as one of the four stages of
creativity: preparation, incubation, illumination and
verification. It is during incubation, that 'resting
phase' of creativity, when those initial ideas from
the preparation stage appear to blossom. Also
related to intuition and insight, this phase allows the
germination of seeds already sown, which can then
be looked at (illuminated) and worked on or applied
or verified. Sometimes, rather than dwelling or
ruminating on something for too long, which becomes
counter-productive, we have to, literally, 'sleep on it'
in order to allow the next stage to emerge. This is very
much part of the process of creativity.

Your creative type

Creativity comes in all sorts of shapes and sizes, and while there is diversity in the ways it can be expressed, there are also different ways to be creative.

How we respond to the information we receive, and the ways in which we perceive, process and organise it, can influence how we respond creatively. The ways in which we do this can be loosely differentiated by what's sometimes referred to as learning styles, and these are defined as visual, auditory and tactile. Understanding this can give an indication of our preferences when we consider our creativity, and how to access and use it.

> **The trick to creativity, if there is a single useful thing to say about it, is to identify your own peculiar talent and then to settle down to work with it for a good long time. Everyone has an aptitude for something. The trick is to recognise it, to honour it, to work with it. This is where creativity starts.**
>
> *Denise Shekerjian, writer & writing coach*

Visual

Those who respond to visual information – the natural world around us, paintings, pictures and other visual material – tend to try and express themselves in similar ways. Or, maybe, they find that doodling is a constructive process when thinking through creative ideas.

Auditory

Hearing sounds, making sense of information through what we hear, can stimulate creativity in the same way. It may be that listening to a particular style of music – rock, classical, jazz, choral, rap – can help the creative response in whichever way emerges, through being engaged with these sounds.

Tactile

Here, being able to physically move, touch and feel contributes to the creative response. The immediate sense of how movement can stimulate this may make us think of expression through creative dance, but that is just one of the ways: it can also include using our hands as creative artisans. Anything from cooking to weaving to calligraphy can give us a way through to our creativity.

Understanding your preferences – visual, auditory, tactile – is one way you can take a first step towards liberating a more expansive creativity. What can really make it interesting, though, is when we choose to move away from our preferences and utilise other ways of seeing or responding creatively to the information we access in these different ways. Look at how these three styles can link and contribute each to the other. Creative dance is often developed in response to particular music. A beautifully made pot relies on the visual eye and the tactile ability of the potter. Imaginative writing can be in response to what is seen. These juxtapositions can inform, enhance and contribute to creativity, so even if you are predisposed to one form of creativity over another, don't restrict your access to the others.

To be truly inspired, you must learn to trust your instinct, and your creative empathy ... Without those, you can still give a good, technically correct performance – but it will never be magical.

TAMARA ROJO, ARTISTIC DIRECTOR & PRINCIPAL DANCER,
ENGLISH NATIONAL BALLET

Quiz

If you want to up your creativity, it's also worth pausing to stop and think about how creative you are now and how you might consider bringing more creativity into your life. Answer the questions below to see where you currently sit with your creativity – and what you might do to help give it a boost.

› **How creative do you consider yourself to be?**
A Very.
B Quite, when necessary.
C Not much.

› **How do you feel about having time on your hands with nothing to do?**
A It's my idea of bliss.
B There's always something to do.
C Bored.

› **What inspires you most?**
A The world in my head.
B The world around me.
C Nothing much.

› **Does it matter to you what people think of you?**
A No, my own self-respect is more important.
B Some people more than others.
C Yes.

› **What motivates you most?**
A Achieving something that pleases me.
B Getting the job done.
C Getting paid.

› **Do you prefer a routine?**
A No, it bores me.
B I'm flexible and can work with or without it.
C Yes, I like to know what I'm doing.

› **How often do you exercise?**
A I like fo walk outside every day.
B I go to the gym when I can.
C Too busy for exercise.

› **What's your idea of risk?**
A Parachuting from a plane.
B Pitching a left-field idea.
C Cycling without a helmet.

> **How would you like to spend your retirement?**

A I won't retire.

B Something creative I don't have time for now.

C Lying on a beach.

> **How often do you mix with people outside your social or work group?**

A All the time.

B Sometimes, but I have to make the effort.

C Never.

Mostly As

Your whole inclination is towards what feeds your creativity. It's an integral part of your life and if you don't already work in a creative industry, this might be something to consider or, at least, bring those more creative aspects of your personality into your working life or studies. You may also need to focus a bit, to make sure that at least some of your ideas reach reality.

Mostly Bs

There's probably a rather untapped core of creativity that you exercise well, but not all the time. What you do also have is the ability to be flexible enough to embrace a creative idea and then deliver on it. It may not be the most interesting part of your life at the moment, but it may be something that could be developed – either within your working life or outside it.

Mostly Cs

Most of what you do can appear to be a means to an end, and creativity doesn't necessarily play much part in it. It may also be, however, something you'd like to explore and find a way to express, in which case it's worth finding ways to open yourself up to the sort of things that feed creativity, which could mean doing things that you haven't considered: visiting an art gallery, exploring a culture outside your own, talking to people outside your usual social group or reading a novel.

Discovering personal creativity

It would be nice to think that there was some formula to creativity, some x + y = creativity, but it doesn't really work like that. Creativity is as much a result of an internal process as an external one.

So how can you discover your own personal creativity? Feeding that internal process is as good a place to start.

And it probably pays to start with something you are interested in and have access to. Much of creativity comes from our imaginations, but your imagination needs something to work with – so feed it. But it can also arise from a general opening up of your way of thinking – and that can happen through exposure to things outside your immediate sphere.

Life is energy, and energy is creativity. And even when individuals pass on, the energy is retained in the work of art, locked in it and awaiting release if only someone will take the time and the care to unlock it. *Marianne Moore, poet*

But start with what you do everyday: whether you are a student, worker or retired, you don't need to make time to spark your creativity; it can run alongside everything else. That boring commute to work every morning? This could be the perfect time to download and listen to inspiring podcasts or music, or read a book. Accessing other people's creativity can sometimes spark your own. Or write a journal, using what you see around you to help focus your observation. Or talk to the person in the seat next to you: we can spend so much time inside our own little bubbles that we forget the value of interaction and exchange.

Then, move it on ...

If you only ever listen to classical music, take some time to listen to some jazz – or at least find an alternative to what your first choice might be. Go and hear music performed live, rather than through your headphones. Do anything that shifts your initial perspective on its axis to open up your ideas. Discovering personal creativity is difficult if you stay consistently within your own comfort zone. So challenge that in any way that extends your personal boundaries. It's impossible to discover interests, a talent or skill without finding or creating those opportunities you need to explore to see if they can be developed into something that becomes an outlet for personal creativity.

Opportunities at our fingertips

The majority of us now own mobile phones with great camera facilities literally at our fingertips, but only ever taking a selfie for an Instagram account is an immediate limitation of what it – and you – could do to make more creative use of it. Then, maybe ... think about how this could be progressed. Visit exhibitions, see what other people have created, take a class and, perhaps, buy a camera that uses film ... and think about where else you could take this. The photographic artist Dafna Talmor, for example, makes collages from hand-cut negatives, cutting out any man-made artefact from her landscapes and piecing them together before developing the photograph, producing visually interesting and beautiful effects for her Constructed Landscapes series.

Photography may not be your thing, but finding your own personal creativity – everyone can do this – means being open to taking the first steps.

When my daughter was about seven years old, she asked me one day what I did at work. I told her I worked at the college ... that my job was to teach people how to draw. She stared at me, incredulous, and said, 'You mean they forget?'

HOWARD IKEMOTO, ARTIST

The benefit of curiosity

Curiosity lies at the heart of creativity. If you think about how the wheel was created, it came from a curiosity that posed the question: what can I do to get this heavy object from A to B quicker and more easily? No creative solution can be found without first asking a question.

The cure for boredom is curiosity. There is no cure for curiosity. *Dorothy Parker, writer*

Ask questions

Children do this without thinking. If they don't know something or want to know more about something, they will ask someone, or even question it themselves, in a bid to work out their own ideas or a solution to a problem. Curiosity is a way of exploring ideas and how we think about them, but many of us grow out of the habit of questioning, sometimes because we're told it's impolite – 'Curiosity killed the cat' – and sometimes just because we get out of the habit.

Write backwards. Start from the feeling you want the audience to have at the end and then ask 'How might that happen?' continually, until you have a beginning.
Lucy Prebble, playwright

Observe

To answer a question, you have to observe something closely to gather the information you need to provoke or satisfy your curiosity. And to do this, you have to really engage with it, often through what it looks, feels or sounds like, extending this experience in more tangible ways. This process often raises questions – of ourselves and others – all of which generates and feeds our creativity.

Creativity is tricky in a vacuum: it's difficult to just get creative without having a focus. Take a painting, for example – any painting but, for simplicity's sake, focus on one of the most famous paintings in the world, Leonardo da Vinci's *Mona Lisa*. Now ask yourself the following questions about the painting, and find out the answers, to extend further discovery and get you into the habit of thinking about and around something:

- Who is she?
- What is it that makes her smile so enigmatic?
- When was this painted?
- What 'story' does the painting tell?
- What medium is used in this painting?
- Why is the painting so famous?
- What do you think of it – its focus, composition, style, materials used?

As soon as you start questioning the painting, you begin to engage with it, to think about it, and your own ideas will begin to surface.

I'm driven by my curiosities.

ILSE CRAWFORD, INTERIOR DESIGNER

Freeing the mind: The benefits of boredom, daydreaming & procrastination

It's just not possible to be mentally 'switched on' all the time – but that's not a bad thing. As Ovid said, 'Take rest; a field that is rested gives a beautiful crop.' And so we, too, can benefit from some downtime, allowing creativity to emerge when we give the imagination time off to experience free association and make unexpected connections.

Boredom

Some people never experience boredom. That's not to say that they don't find some experiences boring, but because of either an innate or a learnt ability, they see a lull in activity as an opportunity just to engage with their thoughts and see where these may take them. This may not be especially creative in that exact moment, but it can lead to creativity, because that hiatus, that boredom, may be a useful prompt.

Julia Cameron, author of *The Artist's Way*, actively promotes doing nothing for 15 minutes a day, in much the same way as another guru might suggest meditating. Cameron, however, just advocates sitting with that 'nothing' and seeing where it takes you. The first time you try this, it may feel impossible: we are so used to feeling that we have to fill every minute of the waking day with conscious activity that we allow no time to sit with, process or engage with ideas, from which seeds of creativity might grow.

~ nefelibata (n.) lit. 'cloud walker'; one who lives in the clouds of their own imagination or dreams, or one who does not obey the conventions of society, literature or art.

Daydreaming

Daydreaming can occur during a period of boredom and is a very good use of it. Daydreaming allows an opportunity to give free rein to ideas, fantasies even, and their evolution. Taking an idea, imagining it, thinking about the possibilities – suffice to say that daydreaming should be a positive promotion of ideas, not a slapping down of them. Seeing, in your mind's eye, what something might look like, considering what you might need to do to achieve it: these are all relevant steps along a creative path.

Daydreaming is quite necessary. Without it, the mind couldn't get done all the thinking it has to do during a normal day ...

You can't possibly do all your thinking with a consciousness (that is constantly distracted). Instead, your unconscious mind is working out problems all the time.

LEONARD M. GIAMBRA, PSYCHOLOGIST

BRAINWAVES

It's not just a great idea: a brainwave is literally a *thing*. There are four types of brainwaves and each one lends itself to creativity, separately and with other brainwaves:

- **Beta** – awake, relaxed and alert
- **Alpha** – under stress, mental concentration and focus
- **Delta** – deepest stages of sleep
- **Theta** – between drowsiness and sleep, when we dream

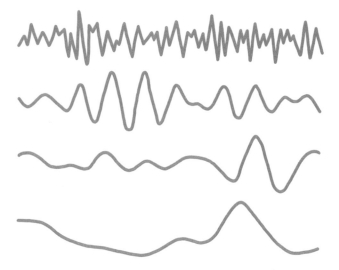

Brainwaves function a bit like the gears of a car: Delta is first gear, Theta is second gear, Alpha is third gear and Beta is top gear. No single gear is best for every driving situation – so, while Theta waves can be good for daydreaming, Alpha waves are associated with creativity, inspiration and peak performance.

Procrastination

What place, then, for procrastination, the potential scourge of the creative achiever? Usually no one has anything good to say about procrastination, or that putting off until tomorrow what you might do today can ever be useful. Wrong: sometimes it can afford you more thinking time to develop ideas. Taking your foot off the metaphorical accelerator isn't the same as putting your foot on the brake: coasting, if you like, can allow you the time you need to consider, formulate and even construct those ideas more effectively. Creativity sometimes needs a little extra space to percolate through and procrastination can provide you with the necessary pause button that your creative subconscious is seeking.

All three together ...

Sometimes you are bored with what you're doing, you procrastinate because of this, which allows time to daydream. This, in turn, frees your mind and allows it to range freely for a period, which can both refresh and reinvigorate your creativity.

Taking inspiration from others

Inspiration means being mentally stimulated by something – something we've seen, read, heard – and it makes us think, perhaps in a new way. Herein lies the germ of creative inspiration. So, on that basis, taking inspiration from others is perfectly legitimate and something that we can consciously aspire to.

INSPI'REIʃ(ə)N/

Inspiration – a process of being stimulated to do or feel something creative, comes from the Latin, meaning 'divine guidance' probably because of the sense that inspiration comes in a flash, apparently from nowhere. The truth is that we can't be inspired in a vacuum. But, perhaps more importantly, it's as well to remember the other meaning of inspire – to breathe in, to inhale air and life-giving oxygen into our lungs. So, in this way inspiration gives life to creativity.

With that in mind, if you want to write creatively, read; if you want to paint or draw, look at what others have done before you; if you want to compose music, listen to the work of others. In every instance you'll need to find out the processes involved – which can initially mean trying out ideas until you end up with something authentic to you. But exposure to other people's work all adds up to creative inspiration.

Inspiration exists, but it must find you working.

PABLO PICASSO, ARTIST

Inspiration ... or copying?

So, initially at least, this might include some copying. Learning to do anything from dance steps to brush strokes starts by copying someone else. Then, when you have the skill, you can develop your own ideas. Your ideas may not be direct copies, but may initially aspire to what it was that inspired them. Ideas may be referenced from other ideas through whatever medium in which you choose to express yourself, in order to achieve what you're aiming for. And, curiously, you can't copyright ideas.

Copying, or emulation, is not a bad place to start and can be a springboard to your own, greater, creativity. If you look around you, you'll see how this has played out over the years, for example in art. Consider the different art movements – abstract, cubism, expressionism, impressionism, Fauvism, realism, romanticism, art deco – all of which had a philosophy and goal common to those who aspired to it. Yes, there were similarities in style, but those great artists whose work has endured were compelled to express something of themselves through their art, even if they emulated a new, or each other's style. They too were also influenced by what was going on around them socially or politically, or the area in which they lived, which was often reflected in their work.

Nothing is original. Steal from anywhere that resonates with inspiration or fuels your imagination. Devour old films, new films, music, books, paintings, photographs, poems, dreams, random conversations, architecture, bridges, street signs, trees, clouds, bodies of water, light and shadows. Select only things to steal from that speak directly to your soul. If you do this, your work (and theft) will be authentic. Authenticity is invaluable; originality is nonexistent. *Jim Jarmusch, film director*

Coming up with ideas

Once you get into the creative zone, coming up with ideas is no problem. But how can you get to that place where inspiration strikes? The truth is, inspiration for ideas is all around you as long as you know how to look to find it. The other thing to realise is that coming up with ideas can be as much work as bringing them to fruition. Once you accept the work involved, then you are ready to work out what will inspire you.

An idea is just a map. The ultimate landscape is only discovered when it's under foot, so don't get too bogged down in its validity. *Rupert Goold, theatre director*

Seek inspiration everywhere

One meaning of inspiration is the drawing in of breath, inhalation, a life force that you take in from outside the body. In a similar way, we are inspired by what we are exposed to, what we see and take in to our own imaginations, from which we can create. Expose yourself to the familiar and the unfamiliar. If you only listen to classical music, listen to some rap: if your favourite artist is Botticelli, then check out some Frank Auerbach. Don't play safe; explore everything and anything that might spark an idea. One of the most inspirational artists and masters of self-reinvention, David Bowie, was constantly refreshing his experience of the arts – from his exceptional art collection, to the diversity of his reading, to his exposure to all forms of music – he knew that to limit himself would restrict his artistic creativity.

I have a magpie attitude to inspiration: I seek it from all sorts of sources; anything that allows me to think about how culture comes together. I'm always on the lookout – I observe people in the street; I watch films, I read, I think about the conversations that I have. I consider the gestures people use, or the colours they're wearing. It's about taking all the little everyday things and observing them with a critical eye; building up a scrapbook which you can draw on. *Isaac Julien, artist*

Specific ideas

Sometimes, however, we need to come up with an idea for something specific – maybe you're working on a project that has to fit someone else's brief, so there are parameters to which you have to adhere – how, then, can you find the creative ideas you need? When this is the case, when you need to work with other people's expectations, you need to do some research first to get a feel for what they hope to achieve. Walk in their shoes as it were, work out what problems need to be solved, what the restrictions could be, who's involved, what's their stake in it all: ask questions – not just the obvious questions but the unobvious – listen to the answers and make notes. Consider all these things, be stimulated by them and then start working out your own ideas.

Ideas are like rabbits. You get a couple and learn how to handle them, and pretty soon you have a dozen.

JOHN STEINBECK, WRITER

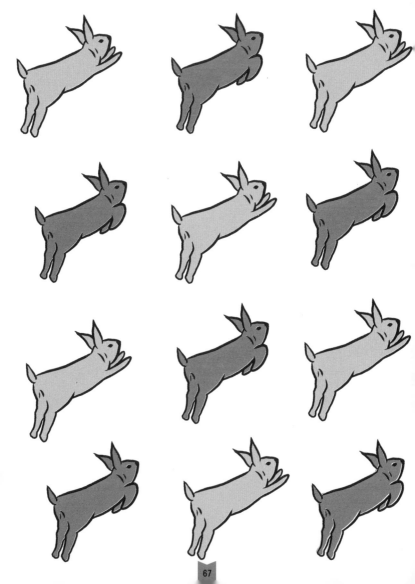

Take a walk

Sitting at your desk waiting to be inspired won't work. Back in 1889 the philosopher Friedrich Nietzsche noted that 'All truly great thoughts are conceived by walking' and a 2014 study from Stanford University proved him right. Using a recognised test of creative divergent thinking, researchers found that the physical activity of walking demonstrably increased creativity. This was not to do with the perceptual stimulation of moving through a different environment, as the same results emerged from walking on a treadmill while looking at a blank wall, but came from the physical activity itself; and this effect continued even after those who'd been walking were sitting at their desks again. 'We're not saying that walking can turn you into Michelangelo,' said one of the study's authors, Marily Oppezzo. 'But it could help you at the beginning stages of creativity.'

The little images that I get from sitting alone in my apartment – the way the light is falling through the window; the man I just saw walk by on the other side of the street – find their way into snatches of lyrics. I write in short spurts – for five, 10, 15 minutes – then I pace around the room, or go and get a snack.

MARTHA WAINWRIGHT, SINGER-SONGWRITER

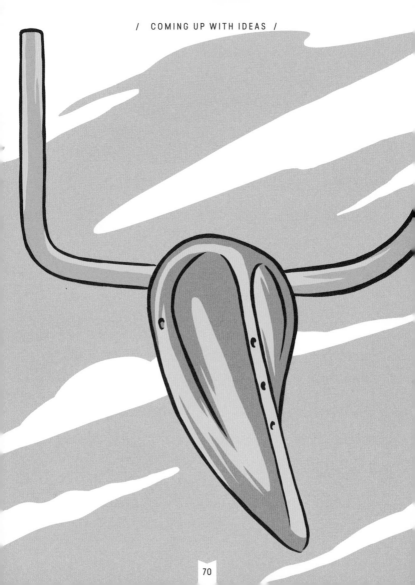

I begin with an idea, and then it becomes something else.

PABLO PICASSO, ARTIST

Creating space to create

The first space to create is the one inside your head. This starts with a frame of mind that can accept the amount of work it takes to realise a greater creativity, whether in your work, personal or artistic life.

How do you get there?

So, give yourself permission; turn off those other voices in your head that say can't, couldn't, shouldn't, won't. Run your creativity alongside everything else you do: they're not separate. It doesn't mean that everything you do is creative, but that you are alert to any creative possibilities. If your creativity is expressed through music, you can't switch the germ of an idea on and off: you have to capture it at the time it comes to you to work on later. The same applies to a story idea, or a formulation of words.

A room of one's own

Sometimes, however, you need – as Virginia Woolf put it – a room of one's own. This was, to an extent, a metaphorical room of one's own and Woolf's book of the same title began as a series of two lectures that she gave at the women-only Cambridge University colleges of Girton and Newnham in 1928, and her conclusion was that women must have a private space, as well as financial independence, if they are to write well.

To be creative in your own fashion requires you to work out what you might need in order to be so. Space in which to create may be physical – if you wish to be an artist, you may need a studio or you may need to live somewhere where you can paint outside, or integrate this with your work, or change your working practice to paint full time. Or it may be that you need to find a group of like-minded people to collaborate with, or, instead, you need a totally quiet, separate environment away from everyone.

Whatever space you need, make a commitment to yourself to find it.

Practising creativity

To take a sporting metaphor, in the same way that you can't get good at basketball without shooting hoops, you have to practise creativity to become more skilled at it. You have to flex that creative muscle regularly, every day, for it to yield results. This in turn will help to build your creative confidence, which is important because it will shield you against put-downs, other people's judgements and that fear of failure that can prevent you from trying.

Learn how to see. Realise that everything connects to everything else.

LEONARDO DA VINCI, ARTIST

Making connections

There are numerous ways to do this, but making unobvious or unexpected connections can help to generate new and creative ideas. Knowing stuff, pieces of information, in itself isn't enough; you have to connect pieces of information with your knowledge to create. Put at its simplest, anyone can learn to read music, but unless you hear it played, you won't know what it sounds like, and if you don't play an instrument, learning to read music isn't enough to experience those creative connections. Without making connections, there is no creativity.

When you take this a stage further and think about how you can fuel your own brain with knowledge and connections, you can see how it begins to work creatively: you then have the substance from which creativity is fuelled. Without connections, information remains isolated.

Creativity is just connecting things. When you ask creative people how they did something, they feel a little guilty because they didn't really do it, they just saw something. It seemed obvious to them after a while. That's because they were able to connect experiences they've had and synthesize new things. And the reason they were able to do that was that they've had more experiences or they have thought more about their experiences than other people.

Steve Jobs, entrepreneur & designer

Relationships

Linked to the idea of connections, relationships that can arise between ideas and things can take creativity further. For example, we now expect to have a music score on a film – something that originated back in the day of the silent movies, with a live piano player in the auditorium – but its use has become increasingly innovative and today it is used much more creatively, to help create mood or tension, and also by its absence. Whether music is used in places during a movie, or not, creates a different sort of relationship to our experience of the narrative – albeit subconsciously. All of this contributes to the storytelling. Seeing the possibility of relationships – or strategic alliances – between things is often key to novel, creative approaches where they are more effective in combination.

Multiple solutions

When it comes to problem solving, it's a mistake to think there can be only one solution. We often have very fixed thinking and until we look at something from a different perspective, our ideas can be limited. Taking a 'why not?' approach can help to yield new ideas. Don't try harder to solve problems: try differently.

The driver of a high-topped truck had underestimated the height of a bridge and had become stuck, being unable to either reverse or go forward, blocking the traffic. As the 'experts' considered how to solve this problem in a variety of ways from cutting off the top of the truck to removing bricks from the bridge, a child approached, watched for a while and then said, 'Why don't you let the tyres down on the truck?' This lowered its height and the truck was able to gently reverse. Problem solved.

Contradictory ideas (mix and match)

Some of the most interesting ideas can arise when we contradict the obvious or when we use an object in an unexpected or innovative way. This innovation becomes a tool for creativity and it's this sort of cross-pollination – perhaps between the arts and industry, medicine and music – that can fertilise new ideas.

Tenacity & discipline

Whether you take an existing idea and make it better or dream up something completely new, whether it's creating Tumblr or Spanx, the difference between the ideas we know about and the ones we don't is that someone just kept plugging away with it until it became a reality. The original idea may come in and out of focus, but it remains at the core of what is explored, shaped and developed. Often it takes real tenacity to keep an idea alive, bringing it to fruition often just slightly ahead of the market curve. Then you hold your breath. But along with that first 1 per cent of inspiration came 99 per cent of perspiration: it seems the old clichés hold true. Tenacity works.

Steve Jobs famously said, 'A lot of times, people don't know what they want until you show it to them.' He famously rejected market research, relying instead on his intuition – and a highly creative team of world-class designers – to produce those Apple products, the Mac, the iPhone, etc., we didn't know we wanted but now can't live without. He didn't give up, but stuck with what he believed.

To become successful at anything, you've got to practice discipline. You must do something over and over and over again to do it extremely well. And being creative is no exception.

STEPHEN KEY, STRATEGIST & WRITER

Tenacity, sticking with something, is part of the discipline involved in being creative. You don't give up at the first hurdle. If it doesn't work, you think about why and how you might approach it differently to make it work. You come at it from a different angle, use different materials, or take one aspect that does work, discarding the rest. This process takes energy and single-mindedness, but at its core lie tenacity and the discipline to stick with something.

Discipline

Although being creative is work, some of what it takes to become creative is also work, a means to an end. It's important not to mistake those crucial steps along the way as being the work itself: by that, I mean it can be very easy to circle an idea for a long time, like flights over an airport, but then you have to land and get to grips with the core of the idea. That is different work, but without it you will have nothing to show for your creativity.

Sometimes the process can take a while, depending on the state of your tools; sometimes it can happen quickly. The point is, sometimes you just have to graft until it happens: and this takes discipline that is, itself, a learning process.

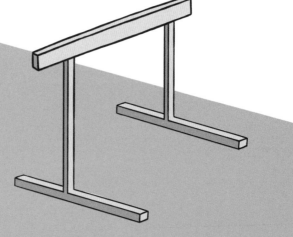

Bottom line? Stick with it.

Sleep on it

When it comes to innovating ideas, problem solving or making those creative connections that seem to come from nowhere, literally 'sleeping on it' can be helpful. Neuroscientists have found that a number of things happen either during sleep, when we dream, or during that twilight zone between sleep and wakefulness – all of which have implications for creativity.

> **It is a common experience that a problem difficult at night is resolved in the morning after the committee of sleep has worked on it.** *John Steinbeck, writer*

Dreams

There's something about the dreaming state that makes it possible to access subconscious thought. This is what lies at the heart of the analytical work of psychoanalysts like Carl Jung and Sigmund Freud, who both recognised that the free-associating connections that occur during dreaming could yield interesting ideas and solutions. During dreaming sleep – the REM (rapid eye movement) stage of sleep – we process information from the day, organising and storing memories for later access. This stage of sleep helps connect apparently unrelated ideas, making new connections between them that can inform creative thinking. It also 'clears the decks' as it were, refreshing our ability to think through ideas and information, especially those that are new to us.

Twilight zone

That hiatus between waking and sleeping has a technical name: hypnagogic state. In this transitional state the imagery in our minds is particularly rich, and this is something that the great surrealist painter Salvador Dali recognised. He devised a method of accessing this state by deliberately falling asleep but with a metal key or spoon held in his hand over a metal plate so that, as he fell asleep, he dropped the key and the noise of its clatter woke him. It is as if, as we enter sleep, our usual mental filters switch off, allowing all sorts of unfettered perceptual and sensory thoughts, ideas or connections to emerge.

This slightly hallucinogenic state can also be induced by other, chemical means. The Victorian poet Samuel Taylor Coleridge was well known for his use of hallucinogenic drugs like opium, which Charles Dickens also used. Sigmund Freud experimented with cocaine, while Dr Timothy Leary experimented with LSD, giving rise to the psychedelic revolution. Alcohol was the drug of choice for Edgar Allen Poe, Ernest Hemingway and numerous others. Finding some way to release the artistic muse by releasing the mental state has long been a feature of creativity, but it all comes down to this twilight, transitional state of consciousness.

Lack of sleep

Without adequate sleep, we can't process the information on which we need to draw. Chronic sleep deprivation, however, means we produce more stress hormones and, in a tense and fraught state, our thoughts can become distracted, making personal creativity difficult. Even though chronic sleep deprivation can also lead to hallucinatory states, the benefits of good, regular sleep are probably a more reliable adjunct to creativity.

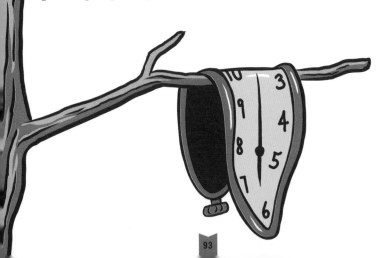

There is a time for many words, and there is also a time for sleep.

HOMER, AUTHOR OF *THE ILIAD* & *THE ODYSSEY*

The creativity of collaboration

Working in glorious isolation is part of the creative process: sometimes it just takes time to sit with an idea, process it and allow it to flourish. At other times it takes input from elsewhere to help crystallise, kick-start or develop something creatively. A creative team is greater than its separate parts, because when everyone brings something unique to the table, the possibilities are greater.

Collaboration provides the opportunity to bounce ideas around, utilise the experience, expertise and skills of others, and benefit from cross-fertilisation of ideas. Different creative resources have different contributions to make because of their specific disciplines, but they can also work together and enhance each other – music, dance or drama, for example.

> **Go on a journey with someone who is as different to you as chalk and cheese. I am inspired by the dialogue between two different bodies, two different minds, two different ways of expressing a single idea.** *Akram Khan, dancer & choreographer*

Mix it up

Es Devlin's set designs for the band U2's 2015 Innocence + Experience tour, the New York Metropolitan Opera's 2015 - 2016 season of *Otello* and Benedict Cumberbatch's *Hamlet* in 2015 are a case in point: her work is a demonstration of the importance of collaboration, where the visual aspect enhances the drama. There's a whole ensemble of people involved, from actor to director to set designer, all working to get it right, to make it work for an audience; and this demands close, creative collaboration where the visual idea works to further illuminate the artistic expression of the work. Likewise, choreographer Alexander Whitley's 2017 work *8M:NUTES*, produced in collaboration with Sadler's Wells, took its inspiration from the stunning images and data produced by solar science research scientists at STFC RAL Space (the Science and Technology Facilities Council's Rutherford Appleton Laboratory), which carries out world-class space research and technology development with involvement in over 210 space missions. Working also with electroacoustic music innovator Daniel Wohl, who composed the original score, and using high-definition imagery from BAFTA award-winning visual artist Tal Rosner, this intense collaboration ensured that *8M:NUTES* was a striking, immersive environment of dance, music and film designed to illuminate our relationship with the star that gives us life: the sun.

Be as collaborative as possible. I do a lot of my thinking once I'm in the rehearsal room – I'm inspired by the actors or designers I'm working with. Other creative people are a resource that needs to be exploited.

ANTHONY NEILSON, PLAYWRIGHT & DIRECTOR

Creativity in business

Collaboration is big in the business world and can work greatly to its advantage. It relies on good leadership to bring a team together, someone who understands what the outcome should be and can harness the different skills and expertise together creatively, so that the team achieves a specific purpose. A team cannot consist of those with the same experience, expertise or views: there need to be points of contention. There's no purchase without a little friction; working with 'yes men' doesn't yield innovation. But with the right combination, creativity can really flourish. Be open to someone else's differing view of the world, as this can provide insights you hadn't considered, and their ideas can inspire your own.

Manage brainstorming

Beloved of many business gurus, this form of collaboration can sometimes be a real time waster. Limit the amount of time spent on the 'brainstorm' stage, then extrapolate three key ideas to work on, rejecting the rest. It has been proven that too many ideas can result in something banal and unexceptional, resorting to the lowest common denominator of mediocrity.

The creative muse

Sometimes the creative collaboration can be with a muse – someone or something that becomes the focus of a desire to express ourselves through some sort of creativity. Inspiration may be internalised into a psychological world and drawn upon, or may happily co-exist with another in real life. We may be inspired by someone else's work or ideas, or we may feel inspired by an individual.

Ethel Person, a renowned psychoanalyst, observed in her work that many people had a dream, 'to find a love relationship which is also the locus of creative collaborative work'. That sort of intimate creativity, resonating between two people, also risks vulnerability, but does so in a way that can release greater creativity. There are numerous examples of couples who have inspired each other, to their mutual advantage and that of their work: painters Frida Kahlo and Diego Rivera; furniture designer Robin Day and his wife and collaborator, textile designer Lucienne Day. William Shakespeare had his 'dark lady', James Joyce his Nora Barnacle and Margot Fonteyn her Nureyev.

The desire to create is one of the deepest yearnings of the human soul.

DIETER F. UCHTDORF, AVIATOR AND RELIGIOUS LEADER

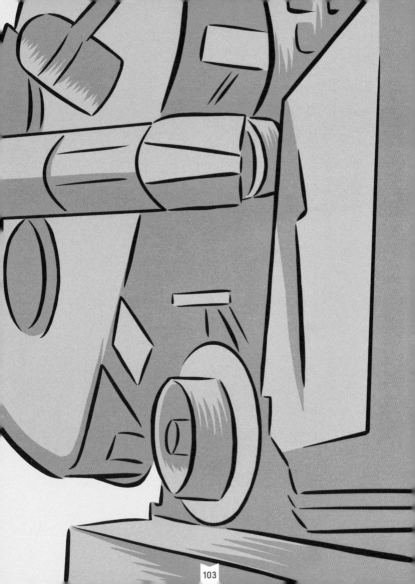

Music

Just listening to music can do pretty amazing things for enhancing your brain's creativity because it fires up so many areas of the brain at once. And playing music takes this a whole step further, purely because the sheer numbers of potential connections are increased.

I always have music on while I'm writing. I'm a very aural person; as soon as I hear a lyric or phrase, I'm transported to a particular time or place. My taste varies wildly. *Polly Stenham, playwright*

How can music – either listening or playing – enhance creativity? According to neuroscientists, music not only fires up different areas of the brain as we process melody and rhythm, it also fires up emotions. When we play a musical instrument, not only are fine motor skills engaged, thereby firing up those areas of the brain, it also enhances memory and executive function and creates a bridge between the left and right hemispheres of the brain. All this neural activity means something of a cerebral workout, and this switching on of connections between different parts of the brain can enhance our creativity in all sorts of areas outside music too.

> **I definitely go into the 'zone' when I play, a mental space no other activity creates. Playing music gives me special insight to everything I do including practicing Taiji (incorporating rhythm in space and time). You know that ukulele you bought two years ago? Dust it off and start strumming again.** Tony Visconti, musician & record producer

Lyrics

When it comes to writing lyrics, being something of a poet – and Bob Dylan won the Nobel Prize for Literature in 2016, after all – can help. And, like writing poetry, at its heart will lie the expression of a *feeling* that is reinforced, or carried, by the music and have to work in collaboration with that. What comes first is immaterial: the creativity rests in them both independently and together.

When I'm stuck for a closing to a lyric, I will drag out my last resort: overwhelming illogic.

DAVID BOWIE, MUSICIAN

Cut-up technique

David Bowie sometimes used a 'cut-up' technique, a way of 'igniting anything that might be in my imagination' for the words that to a great extent formed the lyrics on a number of albums, and in particular *Outside*, about which he said, in a BBC interview in 1998, 'If you put three or four disassociated ideas together and created awkward relationships, the unconscious intelligence that comes from those pairings is really quite startling sometimes, quite provocative.' Bowie was a master of imaginative reinvention, throughout his creative life, but the originator of this technique was Dada poet Tristan Tzara in the 1920s. It was also cited by the writer, philosopher and co-founder of the Beat Generation, William Burroughs.

As with any other sort of writing, keep a notebook, make word lists, explore the work of others, seek out inspiration via the other arts – visual as well as aural. It's all grist to the mill of musical creativity.

Just start scribbling. The first draft is never your last draft. Nothing you write is by accident.

GUY GARVEY, MUSICIAN

Art

A painting is not a picture of an experience; it is an experience. *Mark Rothko, painter*

In a way, there is art in everything, if you know how to look. Sometimes it's there in the colours, or the shapes, or the patterns; in the natural world or the artificial, man-made or synthetic. And it's in how all these aspects of the world around us contradict, juxtapose or sit harmoniously together.

Once you've seen these, or the effect of these things, how are you going to represent them visually, through art? It may be a question of the tools you use – tiny pen and ink drawings, large colourful canvases, the pristine clarity of a photograph or a smudged polaroid, a calm watercolour or digital splodge: how can you use what you have to describe what you see, feel or what you want your audience to experience?

What makes photography a strange invention – with unforeseeable consequences – is that its primary raw materials are light and time. *John Berger, art critic & poet*

Ditch your preconceptions

Think beyond your preconceptions about what you think art 'is', as otherwise this may limit you. The creation of art could elicit the bleakness of a Rothko, the cool tranquillity of an Agnes Martin, the ferocity of Picasso's *Guernica*, the sun-drenched gardens of Joaquín Sorolla, the energy of a Hokusai wave, the pathos of a Käthe Kollwitz, or Warhol's cultural statement of a can of Heinz soup. You can admire the artistry, the dexterity, or just the idea behind it, without even liking it: but it's what the artist's work makes you *feel* that is what makes it creative. It is about this relationship, between the artist and the viewer, which will inform its success. Trying to stay true to that, rather than limiting yourself to an idea of what art 'should' look like will help you to find your way to the expression of your own personal creativity.

The creative act is not performed by the artist alone; the spectator brings the work in contact with the external world by deciphering and interpreting its inner qualifications and thus adds his contribution to the creative act. *Marcel Duchamp, painter & writer*

Doodle

Don't be afraid to doodle, to play with ideas and allow for mistakes. Practise the art of sprezzatura; that 'studied carelessness' that defined the work of artists like Rubens. Art is an exploration, a working out of an idea, as much as a finished product: the work and craft of it is important and this can start with a doodle.

Materials

Explore, experiment and play with what you have. See what your style lends itself to: charcoal, oils, watercolour paint, pen and ink. The choice of materials is as much about the choice of creative expression as anything else: sometimes you need to use the best paper that money can afford on which to draw; sometimes you don't. It's what you do with it that's more important. Be enterprising, be bold and use materials in counter-intuitive ways to express your creativity.

Sometimes the best brush is an old, knackered one: it can take you out of your comfort zone and lead to the creation of something unpredictable and exciting.

JONATHAN HARGREAVES, ARTIST

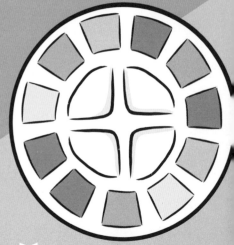

Writing

Every first draft is perfect because all the first draft has to do is exist. *Jane Smiley, writer*

One of the ways in which many, many people express themselves creatively is through writing. And many aspire to share their creative writing with others through publication. But that's not the same thing as wanting to write creatively. Writing for yourself is a wonderful way to explore personal creativity and that practice can lead you places you'd otherwise not go to, through your writing but also where that writing takes you. But whatever writing you want to do – poetry or prose – you have to find your voice, and that takes exploration and discovery, time and practice; however creative you are, you still have to craft and wield the words.

For a writer, voice is a problem that never lets you go, and I have thought about it for as long as I can remember – if for no other reason than that a writer doesn't properly begin until he has a voice of his own.

AL ALVAREZ, POET & WRITER

Read

Probably the most useful thing anyone serious about creative writing can do is to read. Read literary fiction, poetry, prose and essays from renowned writers; read diversely across form, time and cultures. Why? Because in this way you will access and become familiar with good writing, its grammar, syntax and composition, almost by osmosis. It will help you to see, understand and feel what good writing is. And if you are serious about finding your own literary voice, it will help.

Stop reading thrillers and middlebrow fiction. Now. Read nothing but the best, unless you're ill in bed. If you find yourself copying writers you admire, then that's OK. Robert Louis Stevenson called it being a 'sedulous ape'. Embrace it: it's an evolutionary stage. *Alan Humm, poet & writer*

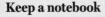

Keep a notebook

At all times have a designated notebook close to
hand in which you can jot down ideas, words,
phrases, references, sights, sounds, names, more
ideas ... you never know when something written
down months ago will bear fruit, shed light on
something else or lead to another idea. But if you
haven't kept a note, it can disappear.

Write in longhand

If you want to change the way you think and try
to think more creatively, change the way you
write and, sometimes, write with pen and paper,
longhand. Explore where this takes you. Many
writers do a first draft in this way, finding the
liberation from the keyboard helps their brain work
in a different – and potentially more interesting –
way. It's almost akin to doodling, teasing out ideas,
rather than hammering frenziedly at a keyboard.

Daily practice

Every day, write. If you are writing a book, even
200 to 500 words a day will enable you to complete
a first draft of something on which you can then
work – within six months. Otherwise you have
nothing to work *with*. It doesn't matter if you reject
in whole or in part what you've written because the
process is never wasted; it is part of your creative
practice. Time is not the issue here; you can always
find a way to make time. Anyone who ever said 'I
could write a novel if only I had time' is lying.

Poetry

Don't fear it. The great American poet Elizabeth Bishop said that poetry was 'a way of thinking with one's feelings'. She went on to say that 'what one seems to want in art, in experiencing it, is the same thing that is necessary for its creation, a self-forgetful, perfectly useless, concentration'. E. E. Cummings, the modernist poet who threw away all constraints – grammar, syntax and form – in pursuit of a new way of writing, dubbed *vers libre* (free verse), stated in one of his finest love poems that 'feeling is first'. So the inspiration for a poem comes primarily from a *feeling*, and one that is crafted into some form of poetic narrative that expresses and describes that feeling in a unique and arresting way, whatever its form, whether it is a sonnet, haiku, villanelle or *vers libre*.

A poem begins with a lump in the throat; a sense of wrong, a homesickness, or a lovesickness. It is a reaching-out toward expression; an effort to find fulfilment. A complete poem is one where an emotion has found its thought and the thought has found words.

ROBERT FROST, WRITER

Tell the story

Whether it's fiction or not, a piece of writing has to convey its story creatively, with a beginning, middle and end, although not necessarily in that order. One of the ways in which writing is creative is in the choosing of what to tell and what to leave out, and how we tell it, in what voice or style or form. That is the writer's job. All these aspects have to be explored creatively because they need to engage the person to whom the story is being told – the reader. Doing this takes talent, but it also takes skill and practice; talent isn't enough. And there is *work* required to achieve this. You may have the tools – pen and paper, or keyboard – but what matters is how you use them to creatively facilitate the information you want to convey.

> **At heart, write always for yourself, *not* for family and friends, for admired teachers, for reviewers or publishers; but make sure you write from your real self, not that one besotted by vainglorious dreams of a future self. One day you will realize that the true rewards of writing lie inalienably in the writing itself.** *John Fowles, writer*

Creative writing courses

These have proliferated in recent years, from undergraduate and postgraduate degrees, to short courses and retreats. And although they can't really teach someone without talent to become a good writer, creative writing courses can allow the structure, time, support, feedback and space to develop as a writer and to actually get some writing done.

Rejection

It sounds harsh, but if you're writing to get published, then rejection will always be a part of that process. Not only will you be rejected, but often you won't be given a reason, so don't expect to get your hand held on this either. Here are some notable authors who were rejected multiple times – Margaret Mitchell's *Gone With the Wind*, 38 times; Stephen King's *Carrie*, 30 times; Robert M. Pirsig's *Zen and the Art of Motorcycle Maintenance*, 121 times. So even bestsellers get rejected numerous times before they are published.

If there's a book you really want to read but it hasn't been written yet, then you must write it. *Toni Morrison, writer*

Sport

What distinguishes a great sportsperson from a good one? The same things – imagination, practice, tenacity, inspiration – that, it turns out, are also the keystones of creativity.

'Float like a butterfly,' said one of the greatest sportsmen of all time, boxer Muhammad Ali. He wasn't known as the Louisville Lip for nothing, and some of his greatest pronouncements provide evidence of the skill, imagination and creativity he brought to his chosen sport.

> **Champions aren't made in the gyms. Champions are made from something they have deep inside them: a desire, a dream, a vision. They have to have last-minute stamina, they have to be a little faster, they have to have the skill and the will. But the will must be stronger than the skill.**
> *Muhammad Ali, boxer*

The beautiful game

When it is played creatively, football, or soccer, is indeed beautiful – taking all that skill and training and using it creatively to micromanage those split-second decisions that need to be taken on the pitch during a match. Not only is a basic understanding of the game required, but also the technical skills and spatial awareness that informs those decisions. They may *look* instinctive or intuitive, but it's an intuition honed creatively from a wealth of knowledge. That creativity doesn't happen in a vacuum.

Creativity in everyday life

There are, as this book demonstrates, a hundred and one ways to be creative, to become more creative, to enhance creativity in your life – everyday, through the things you do for work and those you do for pleasure.

> **Creativity or talent, like electricity, is something I don't understand but something I'm able to harness and use ... Like electricity, creativity makes no judgment. I can use it productively or destructively. The important thing is to use it. You can't use up creativity. The more you use it, the more you have.** *Maya Angelou, writer*

What this book also demonstrates is that, along with the different types, styles and expressions of creativity, there are other factors at play. There's inspiration and the first idea, of course, but there's also opportunity, tenacity, discipline, fear of failure and courage at play. And work. There is always the work of creativity and the process towards this can be as creative – and as rewarding – as its actual outcome.

Creativity requires the courage to let go of certainty.

ERICH FROMM, WRITER

Creativity takes courage.

HENRI MATISSE, ARTIST

Creativity is a way of seeing, a way of self-expression and a way of life. Take opportunities to explore it and its rewards will come, but dispense with any preconceptions about flashes of genius, starving poets in garrets or having a melancholic muse. These may all have their part to play, but, very often, it can take anything up to 10 years to become an overnight sensation. And some don't achieve that recognition until after death – but their creativity, and how they exploited their talent, gifts and work, lives on.

I found I could say things with colour and shapes that I couldn't say any other way - things I had no words for.
Georgia O'Keeffe, artist

There is creativity in everyday life, so be on the look out for it. You may not need to capture the sight of that amazing cloud formation after a storm, the colours of that stunning Pollock painting you saw in a gallery, or that poetic sequence of words you had in your head as you woke, but it is there, informing your daily life and creating an awareness of the resources on which you can draw. Then create your own personal opportunities to do so.

Always be on the lookout for the presence of wonder.

E. B. WHITE, WRITER

Appendix

Further reading

Catching the Big Fish: Meditation, Consciousness & Creativity,
David Lynch (Michael Joseph, 2007)

Creative Journal Writing,
Stephanie Dowrick (Penguin, 2009)

Creativity: The Psychology of Discovery and Invention,
Mihaly Csikszentmihalyi
(Harper Perennial, 2013)

Hegarty on Creativity: There Are No Rules,
John Hegarty
(Thames & Hudson, 2014)

Lateral Thinking: A Textbook of Creativity, Edward de Bono
(Penguin Life, 2016)

Letters to a Young Writer,
Colum McCann (Bloomsbury, 2017)

The Art of Description,
Mark Doty (Graywolf Press, 2010)

The Artist's Way,
Julia Cameron (Pan, 1995)

The Writer's Voice, Al Alvarez
(Bloomsbury, 2005)

Think Like An Artist, Will Gompertz
(Penguin, 2015)

Useful websites

Christoph Niemann
christophniemann.com

Creative Boom
creativeboom.com

Damn Interesting
damninteresting.com

99U
99u.com

The Creativity Post
creativitypost.com

Why Not?
whynot.net

Acknowledgements

In the writing of this book, I'd like to acknowledge all my friends and professional colleagues for those insights and wisdom that have contributed to my understanding of what it means to be creative. I'm also grateful for the continued support of my publisher, in particular Kate Pollard, Kajal Mistry and Molly Ahuja. Working with the team at Hardie Grant continues to be a happy experience – thank you! Thanks are also due to Evi Oetomo. and Stellar Leuna, whose talent for illustration and design ensures my words are brought to life.

About the author

Harriet Griffey is a journalist, writer and author of numerous books focused on health. Along with *I want to be creative*, she is the author of five other books in this series: *I want to sleep*, *I want to be calm*, *I want to be organised*, *I want to be happy* and *I want to be confident*, all published by Hardie Grant. Other published books include *The Art of Concentration* (Rodale, 2010), *How to Get Pregnant* (Bloomsbury Publishing, 2010), and *Give Your Child a Better Start* (with Professor Mike Howe; Penguin Books, 1995). She originally trained as a nurse, writes and broadcasts regularly on health and health-related issues, and is also an accredited coach with Youth at Risk (www.youthatrisk.org.uk).

Harriet

Index

I want to be creative by Harriet Griffey

First published in 2018 by Hardie Grant Books, an imprint of Hardie Grant Publishing

Hardie Grant Books (UK)
52–54 Southwark Street
London SE1 1UN

Hardie Grant Books (Australia)
Ground Floor, Building 1
658 Church Street
Melbourne, VIC 3121

hardiegrantbooks.com

British Library Cataloguing-in-Publication Data. A catalogue record for this book is available from the British Library.

ISBN: 978-1-78488-080-4

Publisher: Kate Pollard
Senior Editor: Kajal Mistry
Desk Editor: Molly Ahuja
Publishing Assistant: Eila Purvis
Series Design: Julia Murray
Design: Evi O. / OetomoNew
Cover Illustration: Julia Murray
Internal Illustrations: Stellar Leuna
Copy Editor: Lorraine Slipper
Proofreader: Anna Halsall
Indexer: Cathy Heath
Colour Reproduction by p2d

Printed and bound in China by C&C Offset Printing Co., Ltd